Table of Contents

7   Masaccio

14   Anthology

21   Plates

62   Essential Bibliography

Masaccio

The atmosphere in Florence, in the year 1401, was one of both serenity and ferment. The terrible war with the duchy of Milan had come to an end three years earlier, and any threat of its resumption appeared remote. The city's government, already strongly molded by the enterprise of the upper middle classes, was able to promote economic growth so effectively and raise its local prestige to such a point that Vespasiano da Bisticci was moved to write, eighty years later: "The city of Florence was in that time ... in a very happy state, overflowing with singular men in every faculty ... each of whom strived to outdo the other in virtue, and the fame of its worthy government went throughout the world, and there was no one who did not tremble at their power." This socioeconomic prosperity constituted the premise and the fertile soil for an extremely varied cultural output, coming from men of genius and great talent whose ideas and different ways of thinking were to culminate, a few decades later, in the great age of the Renaissance.

One of the many significant events that took place that year was the competition for the second door of the Baptistry of San Giovanni, staged by the most important corporation in the city, the guild of the Mercanti di Calimala. The reliefs produced for the competition by Lorenzo Ghiberti and Filippo Brunelleschi lent it considerable importance. The two artists, who both tackled the same theme of the *Sacrifice of Isaac*, approached the work in a completely different manner.

Ghiberti placed the emphasis on expressiveness, on the psychological verisimilitude of his figures; this matched the expectations of the judges and allowed him to win the competition. Brunelleschi, on the other hand, presented a scene whose main characteristic was an unprecedented handling of perspective, a new conception of space. Among other things, he applied for the first time those laws governing the proportion between parts and whole that, once they had been given a theoretical formulation, he was to make part of the rules for the representation of perspective. These laws would quickly be adopted and developed by all the figurative arts: painting, sculpture, and architecture.

The reference to the two main tendencies to be found in the competition entries presented by

Ghiberti and Brunelleschi, tendencies that were profoundly characteristic of the art of that time, can help us to gain a better understanding of the background to Masaccio's training and the role that he would go on to play in the creative world of his day. Born in that same year of 1401, right from the beginning he was able to bring together the best of the ideas that were then circulating in Florence.

First of all the realistic approach to representation, something that was already to be seen in Ghiberti's *Sacrifice of Isaac* and that was then raised to the level of great art by Donatello.

It was a realism that Masaccio combined with accuracy of spatial representation, of the relations between details and whole, driven further and further in his quest for a concrete correspondence between reality and painting by his desire to "imitate from life" in a homogeneous spatial framework and not in terms of the naturalistic particularism of contemporary painting, still in the late Gothic style.

The Early Years. Talent and "Neglectfulness"
Masaccio's short life, lacking as it is in personal details and overshadowed by the greatness of his work (as well as being poorly documented), has given rise to the commonplace view that it was entirely taken up by his love for painting. It is likely that his personality, however exceptional, has been too idealized and it is therefore worth attempting to use the scraps of information that are available to us to piece together a more concrete portrait of the artist.

Masaccio was born at Castel San Giovanni in Altura, now called San Giovanni Valdarno, on 21 December 1401, and was given the name of the patron saint of that day, Tommaso, while his surname, Cassai ("case makers"), derived from the craft practised by his grandfather Simone and great uncle Lorenzo, who both made furniture. Tommaso was the firstborn son of very young parents: "ser Johanni," only twenty years old but already a notary, as indicated by his title, and the nineteen-year-old Jacopa di Mugello.

The only information we have about the first five years of his life concerns the ownership by the Cassai of three plots of land and a house.

In 1406 Giovanni died, and while his profession was a prestigious one he had not practiced it for long enough to leave his widow, Tommaso, and the second son who was born within the year and who was to bear his name, sufficient property to assure their support. Nor was the help offered by the family enough, and so Jacopa, according to an accepted custom, married again within a short span of time. Her new husband, Tedesco, was a much older man, an apothecary who was himself a widower and the father of two daughters.

The second marriage lasted almost a decade, that is until the death of Tedesco. It is likely that the family moved to Florence immediately after this event, although we have no certain information about the date. By this time Tommaso had undoubtedly already discovered his vocation and must have undertaken a kind of apprenticeship, learning the rudiments of art from some local painter, considering that once in the capital it took him less than five years to register as a painter in his own right and to produce a work of such high quality as the *San Giovenale Triptych* (Plates 1-4). It was in fact on 7 January 1422 that "Masus S. Johannis Simonis pictor populi S. Nicholae de Florentia," resident in the parish of San Niccolò Oltrarno, enrolled in the Doctors' and Apothecaries' Guild, while the triptych bears the date of 23 April. The two events should be linked insofar as the painting was carried out on a commission from the Castellani family, one of the most famous in Florence in those days, who would certainly have employed a professional.

Otherwise Masaccio's registration would be incomprehensible, given the taxes to which self-employed artists were subject at that time. The style and a number of solutions adopted in the painting permit other hypotheses to be put forward as well. The first, given the presence of some typical features, is that after his arrival in Florence Masaccio worked in the bottega of Bicci di Lorenzo—who is best known as a fresco painter—where his technique was probably refined and he developed a remarkable capacity for original expression. It is therefore conceivable that by that date he had already made friends with Donatello—at the height of his creativity as a sculptor—and above all with the architect Filippo Brunelleschi—responsible, among other things, for the dome of Florence Cathedral—,

Masaccio

Masaccio

Arnoldo Mondadori Arte

Texts by Franco Ambrosio

Translation by Huw Evans

Andrea Commodi?, *Detail of the* Consecration Feast, *pencil on paper, 25.9 × 30 cm. Ugo Procacci Collection, Florence.*

whose influence is evident in the spatial layout of the central panel.

This possibility is further strengthened by another painting, a fresco of the *Consecration Feast* that has been lost, although several drawings reproducing it have survived. Masaccio painted it around 1424 in the cloister of the church of Mount Carmel, as a record of the consecration of the building that took place on 19 April 1422, depicting a procession of important personages in Florentine life with whom he must have been already sufficiently familiar to have been able to reproduce their faces from memory.

Among them were in fact Donatello and Filippo Brunelleschi, portrayed here in the slovenly attire for which he appears to have been famous.

Masaccio himself, it should be pointed out, cannot have been a paragon of tidiness, judging from the account by Giorgio Vasari who describes him in his *Lives* as a person who "refused to give any time to worldly cares and possessions, even to the way he dressed, let alone anything else; and he never bothered to recover anything owing to him unless his need was desperate," so that, "instead of calling him by his proper name, which was Tommaso, everyone called him Masaccio [sloppy Tom]." It was an indifference—"neglectfulness" was the term used by Vasari—toward himself and others that resulted from devoting "all his mind and thoughts to art," a characteristic that was concretely and immediately translated into a great aptitude for creativity.

The result of this was that reduction of historical perspective in the biographies, to which we have already referred, prefiguring the myth of the modern *bohémien* artist.

A clear debt to the innovations introduced by Brunelleschi is revealed in the design (c. 1423) for the *Liberation from Possession by Demons* (Plate 5), in which the citation of the great architect's work—the image of the dome of the cathedral—is accompanied by a remarkable display of technical skill, used to depict "very fine buildings drawn in perspective; and one can see simultaneously both the interior and the outside" (Vasari).

The outcome of this approach is extremely complicated, with regard to both the system of perspective and the depiction of the episode; indeed too complicated for it to be able to convey the naturalness so important to Masaccio, who probably abandoned it at an early stage to be finished by the assistants in his studio.

It is worth noting the peculiar structure of the temple in this work, which has little to do with the architectural style of Florentine construction and resembles more closely that of Rome.

It was to Rome that he made a journey in 1423, in observance of the jubilee year that had been proclaimed. Masaccio was probably accompanied on this visit by Masolino da Panicale (Tommaso di Cristofano Fini), who had been registered as a painter in Florence a few months earlier, although already forty years old.

The two men had established a relationship of artistic collaboration for some time, which may very well have been based on a feeling of mutual esteem and not, as was long thought owing to the difference in their ages, on a presumed discipleship of the younger to the older. It is in fact difficult to describe them as master and pupil since very few signs of Masolino's influence are to be found in Masaccio's painting—while those of Donatello and Filippo Brunelleschi are obvious—and above all since the talent of the "pupil" was such as to immediately elevate him above all his contemporaries, including Masolino. However the understanding that the two quickly reached was great, to the point of their being regarded as a "precise and well-known duo" (Berti) and recommending them, around the middle of 1423, to Felice Brancacci for the task of frescoing the family chapel in the church of Santa Maria del Carmine in Florence.

The Frescoes in the Brancacci Chapel

The instructions for the construction of the chapel are to be found in the testament of Piero di Piuvichese Brancacci, dating from the beginning of 1367. In his last will, the nobleman urged the foundation of a place of worship in keeping with the importance attained by the family and consonant with the economic resources at its disposal. For not very clear motives, however, the work was not commenced by Antonio, Piero's son, until twenty years later.

The patron of the chapel from 1422 to 1436 was Felice Brancacci, a rich and powerful man and the holder of prestigious public offices. To him can be ascribed the choice of the theme of the frescoes—"scenes from the life of Saint Peter"—out of a desire to draw parallels between certain aspects of his own position as a maritime merchant and the figure of the fisherman apostle. It was however a subject that Masaccio and Masolino treated in strictly religious terms, with a definition of the episodes and a connection between them whose whole purpose was to express the message and the value of divine salvation.

The choice of a single theme and of the same evangelic significance in all the scenes must have raised the problem of guaranteeing the uniformity of the result in its execution, a need that was accentuated by the small dimensions of the chapel—6.84 meters deep and 5.68 meters wide—which make it possible to take in its entire contents at a glance. Masaccio and Masolino, who were undoubtedly well aware of the difference in their styles, overcame the difficulty by means of two general stratagems. In the first place they painted the scenes on the walls in alternation, so that there was no marked stylistic distinction between left and right sides, but on the contrary a degree of harmony. Secondly they worked out a sort of "common vocabulary" made up of schemes of perspective, measurements, and settings, that successfully blurs the formal break between one scene and the next.

Finally it is logical to suppose that, working side by side on the same scaffolding, they were able, by continually comparing their work, to blunt even further the more obvious differences, to the point of achieving the sense of great equilibrium that constitutes one of the fundamental reasons for the feeling of admiration aroused by the frescoes.

At the beginning of September 1425 Masolino abandoned the work and left for Hungary, from where he had been summoned some months earlier by his fellow countryman Pippo Spano. The reasons for his more or less sudden interruption of work on the Brancacci Chapel are not known, but it is easier to suppose disagreements of an economic nature with Felice Brancacci rather than misunderstandings between him and Masaccio, with whom, to judge from the results, there must have been an excellent accord.

At the time of Masolino's departure the parts of the chapel that were already complete were the ceiling, on which the four Evangelists were portrayed, the rear walls, with the *Repentance of Peter* and *Pasce agnos meos, pasce oves meas*, and the lunettes on the left and right with the *Call* and the *Shipwreck* respectively. Unfortunately all these scenes were lost in a fire that devastated the church of Santa Maria del Carmine in 1771 and we only know of them today through the account given by Giorgio Vasari in the *Lives*, where however it is not made clear what was painted by Masolino and what by Masaccio.

That same month of September 1425 had seen the completion of the upper level of the two walls that today, with the work of restoration recently completed (1989), has reappeared in its entirety. Starting from the right, the sequence of episodes runs as follows: *Adam and Eve in the Garden of Eden and the Temptation*, Masolino's *Healing of the Cripple and Raising of Tabitha*, and Masaccio's *Baptism of the Neophytes* (Plates 16-18). Then Masolino recommences on the left with the *Sermon of Saint Peter* and Masaccio concludes with the masterpiece of the *Tribute* (Plates 13-15) and *Adam and Eve chased from Paradise* (Plates 10-12).

After Masolino's departure—the last thing he painted may have been the face of Christ in the *Tribute* (Plates 13-15)—Masaccio continued to work on the lower level, where he painted *Saint Peter healing the Sick by His Shadow* (Plates 22, 23), *Saint Peter Distributing the Goods of the Community and the Death of Ananias* (Plates 19-21), and part of the *Resurrection of the Son of the Prefect and Saint Peter Enthroned* (Plates 24-26). Having reached this point around the end of 1426, with only two and a half scenes left before completion of the

work, he completely abandoned the frescoes in the chapel and devoted himself to other commissions that he had received in the meantime. The precedent of Masolino's departure renders still more likely the hypothesis that Felice Brancacci's fortunes were already on the wane—leading eventually to his being sent into exile in 1436—and therefore not in a position to pay, especially in view of the fact that an artist who failed to fulfill his contract was subject to penalties that Masaccio would certainly not have been able to sustain.

Another fifty-five years would have to pass before the "scenes from the life of Saint Peter" in the Brancacci Chapel would be completed, by the hand of Filippino Lippi.

Taken as a whole, the frescoes in the Brancacci Chapel emphasize the role played by Masaccio, and not only because a larger number of the scenes can be ascribed to him. The fact is that while the episodes in the upper level, executed alternately by the two artists, display an excellent formal equilibrium, they also reveal a difference of quality in which Masolino comes off worse—even though his work is still of an extremely high level. In all the paintings Masaccio succeeds in adopting a procedure in which are blended, in perfect synthesis, the exposition of the theme and the representation of its psychological and moral aspects, an innovative approach to perspective, and the poetry of the settings, whether they are urban scenes or landscapes. But it is in the definition of the figures above all that a level of unparalleled expressiveness is reached, with the realization of "the physical figure of the man that contemporary reflection was indicating as a privileged being, capable of dominating the world" (E. Garin).

Outside the Brancacci Chapel. The Other Masterpieces

The evolution of Masaccio's style is fairly easy to reconstruct, largely on the basis of the stages in his contemporary production of the frescoes in the Brancacci Chapel.

The first step in this process came while he was still working in collaboration with Masolino, and was indeed a commission accepted by the latter and then shared with his colleague since his imminent departure for Hungary did not permit him to complete all the work he had committed himself to. It was in fact at the beginning of 1425 that they started to paint the *Sant'Anna Metterza* (Plates 6, 7), where the term *metterza* signifies that Saint Anne was "placed third" (*messa terza*) along with the Virgin and the Child; the central figures in the picture were entrusted to Masaccio. As well as an unconstrained and modern use of light and perspective—as compared with the central panel of the *San Giovenale Triptych* (Plates 1-4), depicting a similar subject—the most obvious progress here regards the representation of the figures, the ability to present them in all their physical force, as a further demonstration of how the most profound impulse, the main direction of his development was at bottom the "imitation of life."

After Masolino had left for Hungary it is likely that his absence weighed on Masaccio; not only as a friend, but also from the more concrete viewpoint of the large number of works—including the ones to be completed, the ones commissioned from him, and the ones he had inherited from his partner—whose burden now fell on him.

The most important order came from Pisa on 19 February 1426. It concerned an altarpiece for the chapel that the notary Giuliano di Colino degli Scarsi had had built in the church of Mount Carmel. The work is a very complex one, being a polyptych of large dimensions and consisting of around twenty panels. Given the enormous difficulties that would have been posed by its transport, it appears certain that Masaccio painted it entirely in Pisa, spending almost the whole of that year shuttling back and forth between that city and Florence, where he was still working on the "scenes from the life of Saint Peter." There is one slender bridge between these two so different and yet equally demanding works, the small *Madonna and Child* (Plate 32) painted to celebrate the raising of Cardinal Antonio Casini to the purple, an event that took place on 24 May.

At Christmas Masaccio was still in Pisa, although he must already have already finished the polyptych. This is suggested by a document recording, in just those days, the payment of the commission. This document lists, among other things, the many payments on account made by the notary Giuliano di Colino at almost monthly intervals, and which had served to discharge debts incurred with collaborators and storekeepers. They are small sums, but this in itself suggests that Masaccio—who had asked to be paid them—was continually short of cash, even though he was by this time a recognized artist with an abundance of commissions.

Another demonstration of the esteem in which he was held by artistic circles in Florence—where he was regarded not only as a gifted painter but also and above all as a true innovator in the conception of perspective—was the commission that he received in January 1427, on Brunelleschi's recommendation, from Fra Alessio Strozzi, a man of great learning, a theologian, and an adviser to the architect. Masaccio, charged with painting a fresco in Santa Maria Novella, realized what is perhaps his greatest work, the *Trinity* (Plates 33-36), in which he adopted solutions—such as the perfect structure of the perspective that clearly bears the hallmark of Brunelleschi—that were not to be surpassed for almost a century.

A document survives from 1427—the declaration to the recently established cadastre of 29 July, written in his own hand—that offers one of the very rare glimpses of Masaccio's everyday life.

It tells us that he lived with his mother and brother in a rented house, that he shared a studio near the Bargello, and —in some extremely accurate bookkeeping—that he owed forty-four florins to a variety of creditors. His mother was also on bad terms with her relatives, claiming money in vain from both the family of her first husband and the heirs of her second, along with the right to use property.

These are the last events that we know of in Masaccio's life in Florence. The artist was feeling the lure of Rome, with all its attractions and the very different possibilities that it presented for realizing his dreams, not to mention his desire to see Masolino, who had recently returned from abroad and with whom he was already in contact by letter. He produced two more works, a painting for a *desco da parto* (post-delivery dining tray) the *Nativity* (Plate 37) and the lost *Annunciation* described by Vasari: "[Masaccio] demonstrated his understanding of perspective by shading his colors in such a way that the building seems gradually to disappear from view." After this he set off on his journey.

He died shortly after his arrival, and certainly before the end of 1428, without ever having had the time to reveal his true value in that city too. The legend is that he was killed by poison, administered by a rival who had divined just how great a painter he was.

The Legacy

"I painted, and my picture was like life;/I gave my figures movement, passion, soul:/They breathed. Thus, all others/Buonarroti taught; he learnt from me."

Composed as an epitaph in 1550 by Annibal Caro, these words perfectly convey the significance and the role in art that were attributed to him at the height of the Renaissance. A significance and a role that were the outcome of over a century of admiring visits paid by such figures as Fra Angelico, Fra Lippi, Rosso, Pontormo, Michelangelo, and Raphael to the frescoes in the Brancacci Chapel and to the large quantity of other works that were then still in existence. Masaccio enjoyed a high reputation among his contemporaries, but it was during the decades that followed his death that people began to fully grasp the extent of the revolution that he had brought about in painting, by leading it away from the idealizations of the late Gothic and presenting it for the first time with all the visual depth of the natural world.

The words of Annibal Caro, seen from our historical perspective, have the flavor of a testament forewarning of another death to come. The fact is that the image of Masaccio began to fade in the second half of the Cinquecento, obscured partly by the austere and backward-looking tendencies that the Counter-Reformation succeeded in imposing even on the world of art, and partly by the physical destruction of some of his greatest works. As early as 1570 Giorgio Vasari was already concealing the *Trinity* (Plates 33-36) in Santa Maria Novella behind an altarpiece of his own, and this was shortly to be followed by the disappearance of the *Annunciation* and the dismemberment of the Pisa polyptych. In 1600 the *Consecration Feast* was deliberately broken up, and in 1627 a fresco about which we know little, the *Saint Ivo*, underwent the same fate in the Florentine church of Badia. The last threat (1690) was to the "scenes from the life of Saint Peter" in the Brancacci Chapel, when Marchese Ferroni expressed a desire to cover them over, or even remove them entirely, to make room for something more in keeping with the tastes of the day. If it had not been for the wisdom and authority of Duchessa Vittoria della Rovere, nothing would be left today of the frescoes in this chapel but the description in Giorgio Vasari's *Lives*. The very fact that it was possible to contemplate the destruction of these paintings at the end of the Seicento is revealing of the extent to which Masaccio was by this time held of little or no account.

His reputation began to recover around the middle of the Settecento, but only as a precursor to Raphael. It was not until the Romantic age, the reassessment of him made by Stendhal and Delacroix, and the climate produced by Idealism, that his painting was recognized not only for "the precepts and rules of good work" but also for its enormous depth of introspection and realism, that same depth that has led a contemporary writer, Paolo Volponi, to picture him as "he moves around, gets angry, looks at, bangs, and feels the things around him, establishes the dimensions of his world from the corner of a house to a hill, goes back down to the river, meets the fisherman, the beggar, the peasant, with whom he exchanges a few words."

The early decades of the twentieth century brought a recognition of the modernity of Masaccio on the part of artists like Carrà, Sironi, and Soffici, who saw the frescoes in the Brancacci Chapel as the Italian root of European art. This concept of modernity still plays a part in the image of the artist today, reinforced by the discovery that the great capacity for introspection and naturalistic representation revealed in Masaccio's art goes hand in hand with a profound historical and political significance.

Anthology

Before you, esteemed officials of the cadastre of Florence and quarter and district, here I make [known] all our goods and substances, movable and immovable properties, belonging to us Tommaso and Giovanni of ser Giovanni from Castel San Giovanni Valdarno di Sopra, living in Florence [*added:* Quarter S. Croce, parish... (blank), commune of San Giovanni].

We have an estimated six soldi.

We are two in the family along with our mother, who is forty-five years of age; I aforesaid Tommaso am twenty-five years of age, and my aforesaid brother Giovanni is twenty years of age.

We live in a house belonging to Andrea Macigni, for which we pay rent of ten florins a year...

I Tommaso have part of a studio belonging to the Badìa of Florence, of which I pay two florins the year the year [*sic*] ...

We owe to the painter Nicholò di ser Lapo a hundred and two lire and fourteen soldi.

We owe to the gold beater Piero six florins or thereabouts [f VI]

We owe to Lorenzo Adimari and companions 3 florins [f. III]

We owe to Presto de' Leoni and that of the Vacha, for pledges we have made several times, four florins [f. IIII]

We owe to Andre[a] di Giusto, who was with me the aforesaid Tommaso for the rest of his wages six florins [f. VI]

Our mother should have a hundred florins for her marriage portion, forty from Mone d'Andreuccio from Chastel San Giovanni and sixty from the heir of Tedescho from Chastel San Giovanni, who was her second husband [f. C]

Our aforesaid mother should have from the heir of the aforesaid Tedesco the fruit of a vineyard, located in the fish pond, in the court of Chastel San Giovanni, and the habitation of a house located in said Chastel San Giovanni, by a legacy made by the aforesaid Tedesco; we do not write the revenue from the vineyard nor the bounds because we know that none of the revenue of said vineyard [comes] to our mother nor does she live in said house.

[*on the reverse, in a Catasto official's hand*] On the day 29 of July 1427. Santa Croce quarter. Commune of Chastel San Giovanni

Tomaso son of ser Giovanni painter, lives in Florence at San Pulinari in studio, has an esti-

mated 6 soldi.
Registered, paper 71.
(Masaccio's declaration to the Cadastre, Commune of San Giovanni, 1427)

Tomaso of Florence, known as Masaccio, showed with perfect work how those who took their nourishment from anything but nature, mistress of masters, were laboring in vain.
(Leonardo da Vinci, *Codex Atlanticus*, f. 141 r-b, 1483-1518)

Masaccio painter, marvelous man, painted in Florence and elsewhere, died at the age of about 27 [*in left margin by the same hand:* on 15 September 1472 his brother Scheggia told me he was born in 1401 on the day of Saint Thomas the apostle which is the day of 21 December], painted in Florence in the Carmelite [church] a Saint Paul between the Chapel of the Seragli which is where is Santo Croci [*sic*] and the Chapel painted there the story of Saint Jerome, marvelous figure; painted more stories in the Chapel of the Branchacci, and better that was painted by three masters, all good but he marvelous painted in said church, in the cloister above the door where one goes from the church into said cloister, a scene in verdaccio wonderfully skillful to any connoisseur, where is represented the square of the Carminio with many figures. And he also painted in other places in Florence, in churches and for private persons, and at Pisa and at Rome and elsewhere; of those known until his time, reputed the greatest master.
(A. Manetti, *Vite di XIV uomini singhulary in Firenze dal MCCCC innanzi*, 1501)

Masaccio possessed extremely sound judgement, and so he realized that figures which were made to seem on tiptoe instead of being posed firmly with their feet in foreshortening on the level lacked all the basic elements of good style, and that those who painted like that had no understanding of foreshortening.
Although Paolo Uccello had tackled this problem with a fair measure of success, Masaccio introduced many new techniques and made his foreshortenings, which he painted from every angle, far better than any done before. His paintings were remarkably soft and harmonious, and he matched the flesh-tints of his heads and nudes with the colors of his draperies, which he loved to depict with a few simple folds just as they appear in life. All this has been of great benefit to later artists, and indeed Masaccio can be given the credit for originating a new style of painting; certainly everything done before him can be described as artificial, where as he produced work that is living, realistic and natural ...
He was very absent-minded and erratic, and he devoted all his mind and thoughts to art and paid little attention to himself and still less to others. He refused to give any time to worldly cares and possessions, even to the way he dressed, let alone anything else; and he never bothered to recover anything owing to him unless his need was desperate. So instead of calling him by his proper name, which was Tommaso, everyone called him Masaccio [sloppy Tom]. Not that he was in any way vicious. On the contrary, he was goodness itself; and although he was extraordinarily neglectful, he was as kind as could be when it came to giving help or pleasure to others.
(G. Vasari, *Le vite de' più eccellenti pittori, scultori et architettori*, Florence 1568. These extracts are taken from the translation by G. Bull, in G. Vasari, *Lives of the Artists*, Harmondsworth 1965)

On the side of the Sacristy in the Chapel of the Brancacci there are many paintings highly esteemed by artists, and by men of understanding, done by Masaccio, an exceptional painter: from which those who followed afterwards have learned the way to work best in painting. This wonderful artist has taken great care over the depiction of many miraculous deeds of Saint Peter with infinite beauty ...
This figure is admired by men of art, by those who understand and delight in art. It has been portrayed many many times: and all the figures in the work of this most noble artist are not only considered remarkable, and of great merit, but all men of good judgement are agreed in saying that all the best knowledge in the painting of every artist has come from this painter, who has been a miracle in his art. From him have learned—not to speak of others, of whom there have been a great number—the divine Buonarroto, the most excellent Andrea del Sarto, and

Raphael from Urbino, so extraordinary, that style which above all admirable styles is still remembered with honor. And in this the artist is all the more to be commended, in that in his time there was no one to enlighten him as to how to work nobly in painting: who in the darkness of his ignorance, still in the greenest of age (for he did not pass the age of XXVI years) showed to who followed after him the true, and praiseworthy path in painting.

(F. Bocchi, *Bellezze della città di Firenze*, Florence 1591)

Before artists painted without design or coloring, and nothing was known of perspective, front, behind, composition, harmony, invention, movement of the figures, or natural folding of the drapery. Masaccio realized this, it seems, all at once, for in his paintings one always discerns the new principles of each of these things, or at least some attempt, as well as a masterly ease with the paintbrush that was not previously known.

(T. Patch, *The Life of Masaccio*, Florence 1770)

Since antiquity has left nothing, as regards chiaroscuro, coloring, perspective, and expression, Masaccio, rather than the renewer, is the creator of painting.

(Stendhal, *Storia della pittura in Italia*, 1811-1817)

Born in poverty, almost unkown for the best part of his short life, he wrought by himself the greatest revolution in painting that this art has ever known ...

Masaccio enlarged the nature of design: he freed his figures from those wretched and tightly-packed folds wrapped around the body like bandages, that seem to imprison rather than cover it. He understood foreshortenings, and his figures truly have life and movement.

From that time on a return to the dryness of an earlier age was impossible.

(E. Delacroix, in *Revue de Paris*, 1830)

Masaccio shows himself to have been, like no one else of his time, a true adherent to the great and strict laws of composition discovered by Giotto, thereby bringing one glorious period to a splendid conclusion in order to open another with his fine and grandiose manner, which, while it is in one respect still linked to Giotto, in another ushers in and prepares the way for Ghirlandaio, Fra Bartolommeo, and Raphael ...

Like Michelangelo, it appears that Masaccio became oblivious to his surroundings while conceiving a work, in order to find in his mind the expression and form most suited to representing the thought and action of the figures that he portrayed.

(J. A. Crowe, G. B. Cavalcaselle, *Storia della pittura in Italia*, Florence 1875-1909)

Masaccio's fellow countrymen glory in the immortal painter, visitors to the Valdarno approach with reverence the land that gave birth to so much beauty, Italy is exalted in him. But what is the place of the Great Man in the Pantheon of glory? And where is the fitting monument erected to him by modern criticism?

Again his glory is felt but is not defined, since it is only recently, and not openly, and not always, that Masaccio has been distinguished from Filippino Lippi, the continuer of his work in the Brancacci Chapel; there are still arguments over whether this or that work belongs to him or to Masolino; nor is enough account taken, to the right degree of its greatness, of the northern art that formally established itself in Altichiero, before Tuscany.

Throughout the Trecento, Giotto held sway from the banks of the Arno; and his grandeur was a weight upon the freedom of the art of painting. Masaccio, outside Giotto's stronghold, sought the verities of life from other and modern points of aim. His was a new dominion over nature, for it fully revealed the exuberance, the force, the character of things; and humanity triumphed in the art of Masaccio, regained its proportions over a monumental background, breathed, moved freely, and thought deeply.

(A. Venturi, "Un voto," in G. Magherini-Graziani, *Masaccio. Ricordo delle onoranze rese in S. Giovanni Valdarno nel dì 25 ottobre 1903*, Florence 1904)

What none of his predecessors or contemporaries could teach him was the fullness and density of his powerful style, the tragic intonation of his sober and succinct narration, the aspect of his

manner that celebrates the living matter of ordinary vision in the order and with the extraordinary emphasis of his decisive representations, averse to any stylistic modulation that is not immediately suited to the figures and things he depicts, almost conserving their material character. This is the dominant characteristic of his painting, and it is Italian par excellence, in the sense that it presupposes the faith and certitude—inseparable from and peculiar to all the art of the Tuscan Trecento in an objective reality to be objectively represented, even where it appears supermundane ... For this very reason Masaccio's painting stands out as a symbolic embodiment of our ancient Christian spirit, whose greatest poetic and figurative virtue was to express itself, having reached maturity, classically, in complete accord with nature.
(E. Somaré, *Masaccio*, Milan 1924)

The ideas of proportionality between the parts and the whole, of mathematical relations, and of harmony, which were the dominating ideas of the aesthetics of Ancient Greece and are expounded once more by the theorists of the Renaissance, came to them also by way of the Saracens ... This idea of proportionality pervades the whole of Masaccio's work. We cannot grasp to the full the profound influence of the antique in his work without studying it as a whole and also the character of his inspiration.
(J. Mesnil, "Masaccio and the Antique," in *Burlington Magazine*, XLVIII, 1926)

The Florentine painting of the Quattrocento was born from Masaccio, but the artist had no direct followers: this does not result from the fact that, dying so early, he did not have time to create a school; rather, from the fact that his humanity was not imitable, nor his harsh and stern world, by that lesser humanity: his feeling of greatness, of noble and controlled passion, was not of the sort that is passed on.
Thus Masaccio appears to be an isolated giant. He seemed to be an imitator of life, and held a philosophical ideal, of Stoic essence; he seemed a classical artist, and revealed, with his passionate soul, a thousand aspects that could be called romantic; he seemed irreligious, and had an inner life that was one of the most religious.

Everyone saw in him the painter of the Quattrocento, as opposed to the Gothic painter. But very few showed that they felt that Masaccio's "Quattrocento" was in his spirit rather than in his art; very few showed that they understood that, in men like Masaccio, what are greatest are not the works, but the men themselves.
The sculptural quality, the perspective, the immediacy, the heroic appearance of the figures, all that, in short, makes that painting great, is nothing but the expression of an artist, who has felt in himself the destiny of man, just as was indicated by the currents of thought of his time: it is because of that feeling that he was able to innovate.
If humanism had emerged out of a new concept of man, if philosophy had made people fully aware of that concept, art, with Masaccio, had expressed and exalted it with incomparable depth and clarity.
(M. Pittaluga, *Masaccio*, Florence 1935)

And yet, objects the majority, the incontestable fact remains that Masaccio had been a pupil of Masolino. Assuming that he was, then it has to be asked whether an accidental fact of discipleship and only because of the difference in age would have left indelible traces on the mental development of the disciple.
Or are there not enough masters who, when a young man begins to use brushes in an out-of-the-ordinary way, look quickly back over the rolls and then go round saying: "but he was my pupil"! And so would it be a case, that of Masolino, of vaunted magisterial credit? But there is no reason to suspect it as no writer prior to Vasari ever told us that Masaccio had been a pupil of Masolino. And, as for Vasari, who is there who, by some chance, has not been able to read him? What Vasari actually says in both editions is that "Masaccio began painting at the time when Masolino da Panicale was working in the Brancacci Chapel in the Carmelite Church at Florence, following as far as possible in the steps of Filippo and Donatello even though he was a painter." Now this is precisely the opposite of a declaration of discipleship, for the comma between the two propositions is clearly adversative and merits an energetic "but." In short Masaccio did indeed start to paint while Masolino was working

in the Brancacci Chapel (and alongside him, on the same task), *but* (that is, contrary to what one might expect) without showing any affinity with his older colleague; *on the contrary* following as far as possible Brunelleschi and Donatello, his true masters ...

When one recalls that he had registered as a painter in Florence as far back as January '22, it is hard to believe that he had not already been in the city for some years. And where on earth, outside Florence, could an adolescent possessed by the demon of the new painting have been? Perhaps at Montemarciano around 1420? This is a pilgrimage that should be left to those critics who still nurse the hope of finding a Masaccio tadpole, embryo, amoeba, and so on, in order to have him climb properly up all the biological steps of glory. Those who wish to do so are welcome to believe that a young man of genius can develop over the course of five years from the zero of that fresco to the immensity of the "Tribute"; for my part, I prefer to imagine that the person who painted the "Tribute" at the age of twenty-five must have already appeared much earlier as a rare example of precocity; and I am sure that even when he was about seventeen, that is around 1418, there was more than one person in Florence who understood what was going to emerge out of the "extraordinary neglectfulness" of that lad who lived in such an "erratic" way.

The astonishing hope of being able one day to find incunabula painted by Masaccio in those early years must be braced, for now, by looking at whatever of Masaccio, since that time, has been able to pass on, without any delay, into other spirits. If we are not more than inflexible in this search, we run the risk of bestowing the title of forerunner on someone who was really only dependent. And this risk has not always been avoided. It may well be that the value of my research has been to finally clear the decks of the fable of the precursors of Masaccio, a man without precedent par excellence, with the exception of Brunelleschi. So hold fast to the idea, fix it deep in the heart, that if in a Florentine painting toward the end of the second decade one sees light modeling and not modulating, a hand seizing and not passing, a belt tightening and not adorning, a color that steeps and does not cover

or shade, then Masaccio has already been there. (R. Longhi, *Fatti di Masolino e di Masaccio*, Florence 1941)

Each figure arises from and is fixed by its own longing, arranged in a setting that is a true one, represented with a truthfulness that is downright painful by a young man who finds and enumerates his things and who recognizes them, even within himself, and who feeds on and is strengthened by this recognition: his relatives, his friends, the neighboring houses, the trees one by one or in a row, nearby or at the edge, the blue banks of the river, the twin platforms of the hills. They are the faces of the upright men that Masaccio met, or those of beggars and the disreputable, or those of the generous people who helped him; surely the face of Saint Peter is that of the man who taught him, in his youth, and who suggested that he should start to work with paint. Each of those figures, and to an even greater extent each of those faces, is that of a day in Masaccio's life, of a happy meeting, of a trust from which he draws a paternal strength: faces with a coarse, heavy structure, with an open or lumpy forehead, with broad rings of tenderness under the eyes, swollen at the sides to curve onto the loving temple, interrupted by the jutting eyebrows, beneath which opens a deep eye socket, gentle as a shore and yielding, where the brown ball of the eye and the white of its cell set a sad, intent thought, the same one which makes the nape of the neck swell, which penetrates the cheekbones and descends as far as the drawn, earthy cheeks, to the mouths sealed by the dismay of rustic folly. Taken altogether these figures never form a group, not even the apostles located around the gesticulating Saint Peter. On that piece of open ground in front of the arches of the house, stretching down to the river and to the furrows in the banks, each one tells his own story, holds his own chin high, fills his space with his own beard. Their attitudes bind the tale together, which then finds its structures and its cadences in the folds of the clothing in which these country people are disguised, and then in the legs of the young man, in their vibrant strength that brings the whole scene into motion, and then in the spatial intervention of the fundamental instruments of the landscape, or in the

echoing of some color: the lime red, the labored, worn green of the rugged hills of the Arno. Perhaps it is the "impatient emergence" of each one, on his own, his trepidation (so tenderly brought out in the figures of the two naked young men who are about to receive baptism), precisely because it is dealt with on the scientific level of research into perspective, that has given historians the sense of an ideal, of a historical awareness by which, to quote Eugenio Garin, "painters like Masaccio and Piero della Francesca formed and caught in their frescoes the physical figure of man that contemporary thought was indicating as a privileged being, capable of dominating the world."
(P. Volponi, "Il principio umano della pittura-scienza," in *L'opera completa di Masaccio*, Milan 1968)

Masaccio's form was achieved through study of his predecessors and contemporaries, as has been increasingly precisely acknowledged in criticism; but the artist shows that he shared in painting the ideas that others, especially Donatello and Brunelleschi, expressed in sculpture and in architecture: an intense and sharp awareness of the classical world, as a background essential to the expression of a new union of man and nature, and of the greatness of man through the demonstration of his freedom and capacity.
(R. Fremantle, "Masaccio e l'antico," in *Critica d'Arte*, 1969)

Probably trained locally in San Giovanni Valdarno, he would have arrived in Florence, having learned all he could in the country.
Once in the Tuscan capital he voraciously sought out the best new ideas wherever he was able to find them.
His relationship with Brunelleschi and Donatello is documented by tradition, by old records, and by his works. At the start, however, he must have looked carefully at Ghiberti, and this is reflected in the *Coronation*. But already in this relief sculpture and in the San Giovenale Altarpiece Masaccio's individual and unmistakable pictorial vision began to emerge and separate itself from other influences, styles, and directions.
(J.H. Beck, "Masaccio's Early Career as a Sculptor," in *Art Bullettin*, 1971)

In short Masaccio, according to these hypotheses of ours, had worked alongside Masolino, right from the start. This would provide a better explanation, moreover, not only of the collaboration, but also of the unitary quality of the initial design. In fact it is not at all plausible that Masolino should have conceived the compositions of the scenes and then have had to change them at the urging of Masaccio; just as the opposite is equally untenable, that Masaccio should have started work on the chapel as the executor of scenes already outlined by other people.
It is difficult to conceive a Masaccio reduced to coloring a composition by Masolino, author of the entire design already worked out in its elements, already agreed with the client. The opposite, as has already been pointed out, is just as unlikely. If Masaccio had become involved only at the moment when the work had descended as far as the middle level, there would not have been that equilibrium in the chapel that had undoubtedly been planned by the two of them, but a random division of parts that not even the continuation and conclusion of the work by Masaccio could have rendered uniform.
Instead the relationships between the scenes, in their volumes, their handling of perspective, their rhythms, are so balanced from wall to wall, from scene to scene, that it is impossible to conceive of them as anything but a design they worked out together.
Thus as we see it, the sharing out of the episodes and spaces would have given the whole chapel a perfect unity: the two languages, alternating in a single setting, would have been set alongside one another without apparent contrasts, and not just in the horizontal sequence of the scenes, but also in the view of the episodes from top to bottom, from one level to another, giving rise to a unity that was absolutely necessary if confusion or clashes were to be avoided.
Not an entire wall by Masaccio and an entire one by Masolino on the other side, contrasting with one another, but both mutually inserted in a text that was given its visual coherence by the brightness of the color, by the clarity of the expressions assembled in patterns and movements of precisely established alternate correspondences.
(O. Casazza, "La Cappella Brancacci dalle origini a oggi," in *La Cappella Brancacci*, Milan 1990)

1

1-4. San Giovenale Triptych,
1422, panel, 108 × 153 cm.
Parish church of San Pietro, Cascia
di Reggello.
Discovered and published only recently
(1961), the work—perhaps the earliest
that can be attributed to Masaccio—
was painted on commission from the
Florentine family of the Castellani.
It was kept in the Basilica of San
Lorenzo at least until 1436 and then

transferred to San Giovenale, in the
quarter where the family had extensive
property. However the long period of
time that it was on display in the city
is indicative of the highly innovative
contents of the triptych, and in
particular of the central compartment
in which the Madonna and Child,
who is eating a grape (a symbol of the
Eucharist), the throne, and the two
angels in the role of servers form a

group in which the treatment of
perspective is unheard of for those
times.
On the other hand the two side panels,
respectively depicting Saints
Bartholomew and Blaise on the left
and Saints Juvenal and Anthony
Abbot on the right, in spite of an
already evident tendency toward the
"natural," are clearly influenced by
late fourteenth-century art.

5

5. Liberation from Possession
by Demons, *c. 1423, panel,*
115 × 106 cm.
Johnson Collection, Philadelphia.
Some experts regard the painting as
an early exercise by Masaccio based on
the principles of perspective that had
just been proposed by Filippo
Brunelleschi, an exercise that he
quickly abandoned and left to a studio

assistant, Andrea di Giusto, to
complete.
The citation of Brunelleschi also
extends to the dome in the picture, an
obvious reference to that of Florence
Cathedral.
The picture is divided up into three
episodes: starting from the left, the
first depicts the scene where Christ says
"Render therefore unto Caesar the

things which are Caesar's"; in the
middle a father presents to Christ his
small son suffering from convulsions;
lastly, on the right, Jesus is again
depicted surrounded by the apostles.
This division into three parts and the
groups of figures have been seen as an
antecedent of, or perhaps even a trial
for the Tribute *(Plates 13-15) in the*
Brancacci Chapel.

6

6, 7. Saint Anne (Sant'Anna Metterza), *c. 1424-1425, panel, 175 × 103 cm. Uffizi, Florence. Confining our attention to the figures of the Madonna and Child, which the critics are unanimous in attributing to Masaccio, we note a more marked* tendency to *"imitation of life and emphasis of the figures" than in the central panel of the* San Giovenale Triptych *(Plates 1-4), depicting a similar subject. A comparison can also be made with Gentile da Fabriano's* Quaratesi Madonna, *dating from* *the same period, but only to show how Masaccio's figures are the complete opposite of Gentile's—here one finds great concreteness and humanity, there absolutely hieratic poses and features—in a contrast that may even be considered deliberate.*

8

8. *The Brancacci Chapel, view of the
left-hand wall. Santa Maria del
Carmine, Florence.*

9

*9. The Brancacci Chapel, view of the
right-hand wall. Santa Maria del
Carmine, Florence.*

10-12. Adam and Eve chased from Paradise, *c. 1424-1425, fresco, 214 × 90 cm. Santa Maria del Carmine, Brancacci Chapel, Florence.*

The position of the fresco, directly opposite Masolino's Adam and Eve, *makes possible an immediate grasp of the great difference in the representation of emotion between the two works. In fact, where Masolino paints "late-Gothic" figures, of barely hinted-at expressiveness, Masaccio is already depicting intense drama and sorrow in the "Renaissance manner," giving his figures attitudes that are clearly those of true suffering. The device of the angel pointing the way into shameful exile while seated astride a bright red cloud adds a further touch of gravity.*

The scene is one of those that were most badly damaged in the fire of 1771, although the very recent restoration has been able to bring back much of its original character, including the total nudity of Adam, which had been covered up around 1652 by leaves that patently had nothing to do with the rest of the painting.

10

13

13-15. The Tribute, *c. 1425,*
fresco, 247 × 597 cm. Santa Maria
del Carmine, Brancacci Chapel,
Florence.
The episode—the most famous
of the whole cycle—commences from
the middle, where a tax collector
demands from Christ and the apostles
the tribute money required for entry
into Capernaum.
Jesus then indicates to Peter the waters

of the lake of Gennesaret in which the
apostle catches the fish with the coin
miraculously in its mouth. This is then
handed over, on the right, in payment
of the tax.
Until the work of restoration was
completed in 1989, it was believed
that Christ's head was the work of
Masolino, and that this in fact
represented the starting point for
Masaccio, who had constructed the

rest of the scene around it. Now
however, the restored pictorial
definition suggests that it is all
Masaccio's work. According to a
recent analysis, he is responsible
for the conception of the entire
composition, arranging the perspective
to take into account the viewpoint of
the observer in the chapel, so that the
picture appears to be an extension
of the actual space.

14

16

16-18. The Baptism of the
Neophytes, *c. 1424-1425,
fresco, 247 × 172 cm.
Santa Maria del Carmine, Brancacci
Chapel, Florence.
The scene was already famous in the
Renaissance, above all for the high* quality of the drawing ("among the
other figures, there is one that
trembles, that is marvelous to behold")
and for its handling of light and
water effects. In the past it has been
considered the work of several
hands—Masolino for the landscape and the head of Saint Peter, Filippino
Lippi for the two bystanders on the
left—but the critics are now
sufficiently in agreement in
attributing the entire composition
to Masaccio, who completed it in
ten days of work.

19

19-21. Saint Peter Distributing the Goods of the Community and the Death of Ananias, *c. 1426-1427, fresco, 232 × 157 cm. Santa Maria del Carmine, Brancacci Chapel, Florence. In this scene Masaccio combines two episodes from the same story* (Acts of the Apostles, *IV, 32-37, V, 1-11): Saint Peter distributing the goods and Ananias's death after being condemned by the apostle for his false declaration of the proceeds from the sale of a possession. The setting is faithful to the Gospel text, with a rural backdrop to the houses, since the verse of the* Acts *speaks of "lands or houses." It has also been suggested that the picture contains a reference to the family of the patron, with the figure kneeling behind Saint Peter being seen as Reinaldo or Tommaso Brancacci as cardinal. As well as the theological significance of punishment for bearing false witness, it is fairly likely that there is a reference here to the establishment of the Cadastre in Florence, to which everyone had to declare their exact income to arrive at a more equitable sharing of taxes.*

22

22, 23. Saint Peter healing the Sick by His Shadow, *c. 1426, fresco, 232 × 162 cm. Santa Maria del Carmine, Brancacci Chapel, Florence. Another episode taken from the* Acts of the Apostles *(V, 12-15) and one that follows immediately after the* Saint Peter Distributing the Goods of the Community *and the* Death of Ananias*: "And by the hands of the apostles were many signs and wonders wrought among the people" so that "they brought forth the sick into the streets, and laid them on beds and couches, that at the least the shadow of Peter passing by might overshadow some of them."*
The four figures standing behind Saint Peter have been recognized as portraits, commencing with the one in a red hood which is thought to be Masolino with the addition of a beard and moustache, while Donatello comes last, with folded hands and made to look old and hoary. Opinion is divided over the others. The blond Saint John is supposed to have the appearance of Masaccio himself, apart from the color of the hair, but there are also those who believe that it more closely resembles his brother Scheggia who, among other things, had the same name as the saint.

24

24-26. The Resurrection
of the Son of the Prefect and
Saint Peter Enthroned, *c. 1427,
fresco 232 × 597 cm. Santa Maria
del Carmine, Brancacci Chapel,
Florence.*
*Unlike the others, all derived from the
Gospels, this "story" is taken from the*
Legenda Aurea *and tells of the*
miracle wrought by Saint Peter at
Antioch, where he revived the son of
the prefect Theophilus, who had been
dead for fourteen years. The prodigy
brings about the conversion of the
prefect who has a splendid church
built, in the middle of which Peter sits,
enthroned, for seven years. The fresco
was left incomplete by Masaccio and
was finished, fifty-five years later,
by Filippino Lippi, who is responsible
for much of the central group with the
resurrected boy and four of the five
figures on the far left. On the other
side, standing by the figure of Peter,
can be recognized Filippo Brunelleschi,
Leon Battista Alberti, a self-portrait of
Masaccio, and Masolino.*

28

27. Pisa Polyptych: Enthroned Madonna with Child and Angels, *1426, panel, 135 × 73 cm. National Gallery, London.*
When still in one piece, the polyptych, on which Masaccio's brother Giovanni and Andrea di Giusto collaborated, was located on the altar of the chapel that the notary Giuliano di Colino degli Scarsi from San Giusto had built in the church of Mount Carmel in

Pisa. Originally it was made up of some twenty panels of different sizes, but it was broken up around the end of the sixteenth century and so far only eleven of its elements have been traced, scattered among different collections.
Reconstruction of the polyptych, along with the exact position of the paintings, has been possible on the basis of the detailed description of it

given by Giorgio Vasari, whose comment with regard to some of the images that have been lost was that they were "very vivacious and animated."

28. Pisa Polyptych: Crucifixion with the Virgin, Mary Magdalen, and Saint John, *1426, panel, 83 × 63 cm. Galleria Nazionale di Capodimonte, Naples.*

29. Pisa Polyptych: The
Adoration of the Magi, *1426,
panel, 21 × 61 cm. Staatliche
Museen, Berlin.*

30. Pisa Polyptych: Martyrdom
of Saint Peter and Saint John the
Baptist, *1426, panel, 21 × 61 cm.
Staatliche Museen, Berlin.*

29

30

LA CAPPELLA BRANCACCI

IL RESTAURO DELLA CAPPELLA BRANCACCI

orario: 10-17 feriali; 13-17 festivi
chiuso martedì
L. 5.000 (interi) - 2.500 (ridotti)

Felice Brancacci, fiorentino, ricco mercante di sete, affidò a Masolino, intorno alla fine del 1424 o ai primi del 1425, la decorazione della Cappella di famiglia nella duecentesca chiesa di S. Maria del Carmine.

Masolino chiamò a collaborare all'incarico di raffigurarvi il ciclo delle *Storie di San Pietro* il conterraneo e amico Masaccio, nato a San Giovanni Valdarno nel 1401 e scomparso a Roma a soli 27 anni. Il lavoro dei due maestri si svolse sul piano dell'accordo e della collaborazione anche se in piena autonomia, rivelando un modo nuovo di interpretare la storia sacra e la storia dell'uomo.

Nel 1425, allontanatosi Masolino, Masaccio continuò il ciclo da solo interrompendo e riprendendo il lavoro fino alla sua morte.

Negli anni fra il 1481 e il 1485 sarà poi Filippino Lippi a integrare, nel pieno rispetto della severità masaccesca, le parti ancora mancanti del ciclo, portando a termine uno dei più alti esempi dell'arte quattrocentesca.

Dopo vari interventi di pulitura degli affreschi, avvenuti durante il corso dei secoli, l'ultimo grande restauro, terminato del 1990 e curato dal Ministero dei Beni Culturali e Ambientali con il sostegno finanziario della Olivetti, ha fatto emergere due novità di grande rilievo: il ritrovamento di alcuni frammenti della decorazione quattrocentesca (come le due teste angeliche e la probabile *Crocefissione di San Pietro* nella paretina absidale) e una nuova lettura del ciclo. Il Masaccio monocromo "cede il passo a un pittore di ben più chiaro e luminoso colore". La differenza fra il "tardogotico" Masolino e il "rinascimentale" Masaccio non appare così radicalmente profonda come si era creduto prima del restauro.

Nella Cappella sono state ricollocate la parte inferiore dell'altare settecentesco liberato dal tabernacolo, che è visibile nella sala capitolare e l'icona raffigurante la *Madonna del popolo* databile intorno al 1268, anno di fondazione della Chiesa, e attribuita al pittore fiorentino Coppo di Marcovaldo.

La Cappella Brancacci, nella Chiesa di S. Maria del Carmine, con ingresso da piazza del Carmine n. 14, è raggiungibile col bus, linee n. 6 e n. 11 in partenza da piazza S. Marco e piazza del Duomo, n. 15 in partenza da piazza S. Marco, piazza del Duomo e piazza S. Firenze, n. 36 e n. 37 in partenza da piazza Stazione.

Informazioni: Centro Mostre, tel. 055/211876 - 212931 - 212195
Cappella Brancacci, tel. 055/2382195

32

31. Pisa Polyptych: Saint Paul,
1426, panel, 51 × 30 cm. Museo
Nazionale, Pisa.

32. The Madonna and Child
(Madonna del solletico), 1426,
panel, 24 × 18 cm. Palazzo Vecchio,
Florence.
Painted for private use (a gift to
Cardinal Casini on the occasion of his
being raised to the purple on 24 May
1426), the picture was long the subject
of debate, not having been mentioned
by any writer of the past, before being

unanimously accepted as the work
of Masaccio.
The decisive factors in the attribution
of the work to Masaccio include the
strong stylistic affinities with the
central element of the Pisa Polyptych
(Plates 27-31), and in particular the
left hand of the Virgin, which is
depicted in an almost identical
position.

34

33-36. The Trinity, c. 1426-1428, fresco, 667 × 317 cm. Santa Maria Novella, Florence.
As well as a dedication to the Trinity, recent interpretations have seen in the composition an allusion to the double chapel of Golgotha: the one at the top of the mountain, with Christ crucified, and the lower one, where the tomb of Adam is located, symbolized here by the skeleton and the motto written above it: "I was once what you are and what I am you will become." The Madonna and Saint John again play the role of intercessors for the souls of the faithful gathered in prayer (perhaps the client and his wife). Painted by Masaccio over two earlier frescoes, the Trinity, a true benchmark of Renaissance art, was itself covered over in 1570 by Vasari's panel depicting the Madonna del Rosario. Rediscovered in 1861, it was detached and transferred onto the counter facade of the basilica. It was replaced in its original position in 1952.

37

*37. The Nativity, c. 1427-1428,
panel, ∅ 56 cm. Staatliche Museen,
Berlin.*
*Attributed to the painter by a
considerable number of critics, it is
one of the very few known works by
Masaccio depicting a profane subject,
and was probably the first delivery
table of circular shape instead of the
traditional polygon. It portrays the
interior of "a fine house in the style
of Brunelleschi" and is "an expression
of that Florentine life that had already
been caught by the artist in the*
Consecration Feast *of the Carmelite
church."*

Essential Bibliography

F. Monti, G. Tancredi, *Masaccio*, Rome 1662.

G. Pelli, "Elogio di Masaccio," in *Elogi degli uomini illustri toscani*, II, Florence 1782.

O. H. Giglioli, *Masaccio*, Florence 1921.

E. Somarè, *Masaccio*, Milan 1924.

M. Pittaluga, *Masaccio*, Florence 1935.

R. Longhi, *Fatti di Masolino e di Masaccio*, Florence 1941.

L. Berti, *Masaccio*, Milan 1964.

U. Procacci, *Masaccio e la Cappella Brancacci*, Florence 1965.

L. Berti, *L'opera completa di Masaccio*, Milan 1968.

L. Berti, *Masaccio*, Milan 1988.

U. Baldini, O. Casazza, *La Cappella Brancacci*, Milan 1990.

Photograph Credits
Jörg P. Anders, Berlin
Elemond Archives, Milan
Mario Quattrone, Florence
Scala, Florence

Printed for Arnoldo Mondadori Arte
by Fantonigrafica - Elemond Editori Associati